Why leggings a

Mary Schoeser

This book looks at the qualities of the material called Lycra®. It explains why this material is particularly suitable for making skin-tight clothing.

If you are using the book to find out particular facts about leggings or Lycra®, you do not have to read it all. Look at the **contents** (below) or the **index** (at the back) to find the best pages to help you. Then just read as much as you need to read.

The basic facts are given in big print, and more detailed information is in smaller print.

Contents

1 What are leggings?

Leggings are garments like trousers, but they are close-fitting and they pull on. They can stop at the knee or be longer. They can be plain or brightly coloured.

If you think of all the leggings you have seen in shops or in magazines, you will know that they come with many different patterns on them, or in many different plain colours.

Leggings are always the same simple shape, with no zip or button fastenings. To be pulled on, they must be stretchy, and this means that they fit closely.

The first leggings

Leggings got their name because they cover the legs. They were first worn by dancers, who needed to keep their muscles warm during the waiting time in rehearsals.

Their way of dressing was adopted by people in keep-fit classes, and this helped to make them fashionable.

Leggings serve the same purpose for dancers as sweat pants do for athletes, but they have to be close-fitting so that the dancers can still move freely with them on.

Leggings are useful garments for dancers.

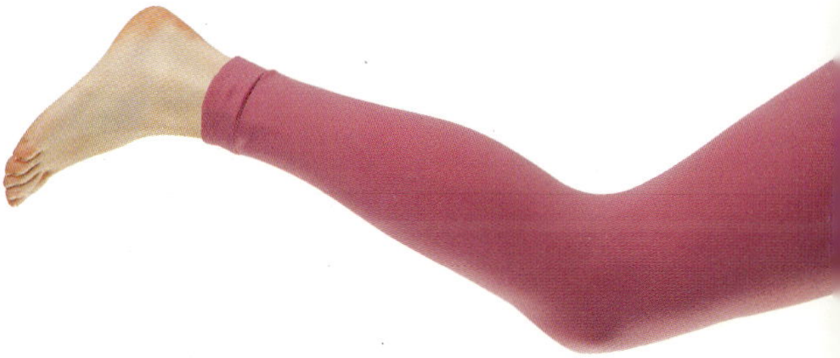

2 What other clothes are like leggings?

Like many other garments, leggings were originally made for athletic activities, and then became a part of fashion. Cycling shorts have also become fashionable.

Tight-fitting clothes were often first made especially for athletes, and then for amateurs. This is what happened with ski clothes and swimwear. The tight-fitting 'body' worn by women was developed from the dancer's leotard, which first became a fashion garment in the late 1960s.

Sportswear in fashion

There are lots of items of athletic clothing that people wear even when they are not taking part in a sport. These include jogging suits, baseball caps and running shoes. Many people wear rugby and football shirts too.

Sometimes these clothes represent a favourite team or sport, but they can also be a way of linking up with an image created by a band or by a well-known person.

Cycling shorts became fashionable in the 1980s. Like leggings, they are also tight and stretchy.

3 Why are some action clothes tight?

Tight clothes are worn by athletes because they might need to move freely, like dancers. They might also need to move very quickly, like cyclists.

A speedskater wears special tight-fitting clothes, but ice dancers wear loose costumes, because they are not skating against the clock.

All the clothes worn by athletes who participate in speed sports are tight. They are like a second skin. This is because these athletes need to reduce any surfaces that will catch the wind or water and slow them down. This slowing-down effect is called 'drag'.

A second skin

Dancing is not a speed sport, but dancers also wear leggings that are like a second skin. This is because the line and shape of their legs must be seen.

The tightness also helps the audience to see the intricate movements they are making. Other performers, like acrobats and trapeze artists, also wear clothes that are like second skins.

↑ Acrobats also wear tight clothes so that they can ensure ease of movement.

4 How do tight clothes move?

Clothes that are skin-tight move freely only if they are stretchy. This is why we say that they are like a second skin, because our skin is stretchy too.

There is more than one way of making the things we wear stretchy. Knitting is a way of making stretchy fabric.

Soft leather is slightly stretchy, because it is made from animal skin.

A natural substance that is very stretchy is rubber, which comes from the sap of two types of trees.

Gloves are knitted or made of leather because they must be stretchy. If they were not stretchy, it would be hard to move the fingers.

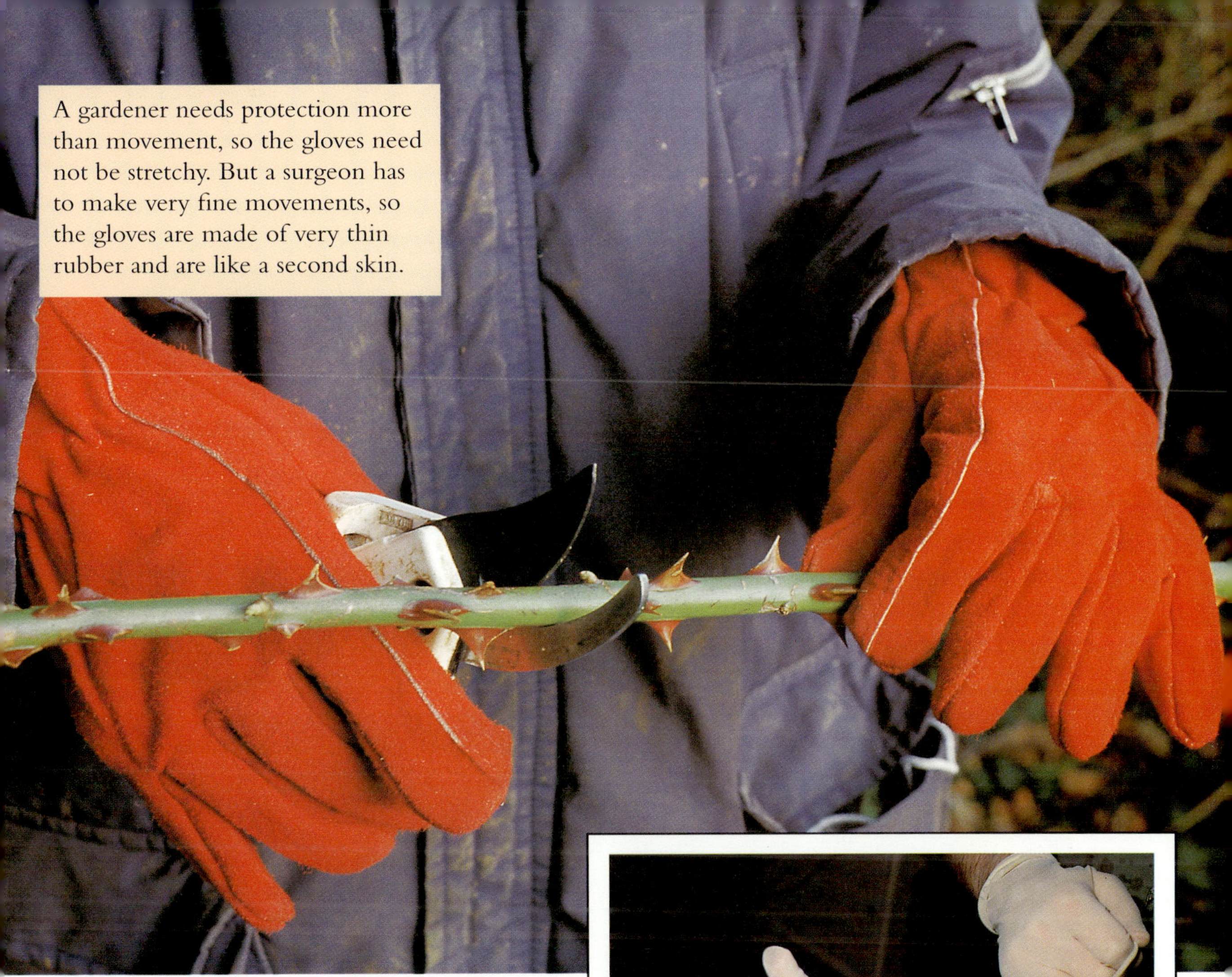

A gardener needs protection more than movement, so the gloves need not be stretchy. But a surgeon has to make very fine movements, so the gloves are made of very thin rubber and are like a second skin.

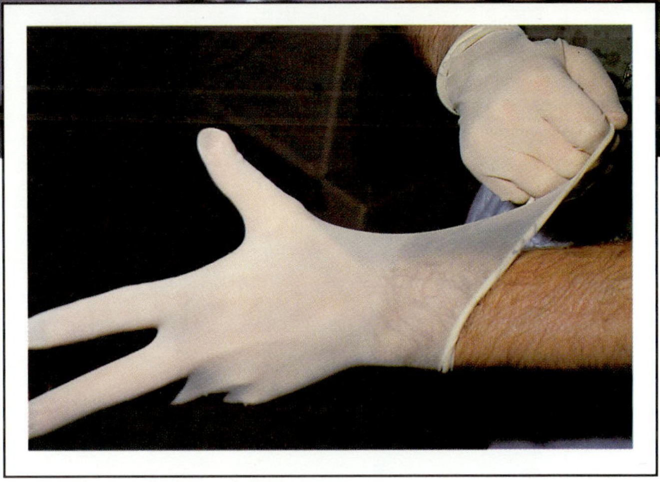

Where rubber comes from

There are two kinds of rubber trees. They both produce a milky sap called 'latex'. Rubber is made from this sap.

The first rubber trees grown for latex were cultivated in Brazil. Seeds from some of these trees were brought to Kew Gardens, near London, in 1876. Seedlings from rubber trees grown at Kew were sent to Ceylon [now Sri Lanka] to start new rubber plantations. From Ceylon they spread throughout Asia.

The second rubber tree, which is slightly different, grows in India and Malaysia, and here it is called the rubber plant. This is the same plant that grows as a house plant in Britain.

5 What is elastic?

When something is elastic, it can return to its original shape after it has been stretched. Skin, leather, knitting, and rubber are all elastic.

We rely on many things that are elastic because they are made of rubber. Tyres are rubber. Rubber belts are often used to transfer power from one part of a machine to another. Other things that have been made from rubber include protective clothing, such as rubber galoshes, which were used as early as 1830.

The Latin name of the rubber plant is *Ficus Elastica*.

This all-in-one synthetic rubber wet suit keeps the diver dry and offers him or her protection against rough surfaces.

A new kind of rubber

During the Second World War rubber was very difficult to get, so scientists developed synthetic rubber, which is made from chemicals. It does not rot like real rubber, so it is especially good in the damp and wet.

Finding out how to make synthetic rubber led the scientists to invent yarns with similar elastic qualities. These are called 'elastane yarns'. If you include elastane in a firm woven fabric, such as denim, it makes it stretchy.

6 What are leggings made of?

Leggings are made of machine-knitted fabric. Many are made of a combination of yarns, including an elastic yarn such as Lycra®.

If you look at the labels inside your leggings, you will find that the most common ingredients are cotton, polyester, and elastane. Cotton and polyester are used because these fibres are easy to wash, and they also dry quickly. Without the elastane, the leggings will still be stretchy, but they will go baggy after a while.

The labels inside your leggings tell you what they are made of.

The baggy leggings are made just of cotton, but the others are of cotton and Lycra®.

Each of these threads is a different thickness of elastane.

About elastane

Elastane yarns are very fine, strong and elastic. However garments cannot be made only out of elastane yarn.

Sometimes elastane is woven with other yarns to make fabric. At other times elastane is combined with other fibres to make a single yarn. This is then woven into a fabric. Combining elastane with other fibres involves special processes called 'core-spinning' and 'covering'.

In America, elastane is called 'spandex'.

7 What is Lycra®?

Lycra® is a trademark for an elastane fibre. The name belongs to the manufacturers of Lycra®, Du Pont. It always has a mark after it, made from the letter 'R' and a circle. No one can use this name without the permission of Du Pont.

Lycra® is a very sheer, thin, and light elastic yarn. It is made from chemicals, most of which come from petroleum products. It can be washed and dried very easily, so it is ideal for garments that are worn close to the body. It is always used with other fibres. Lycra® has been available since 1958.

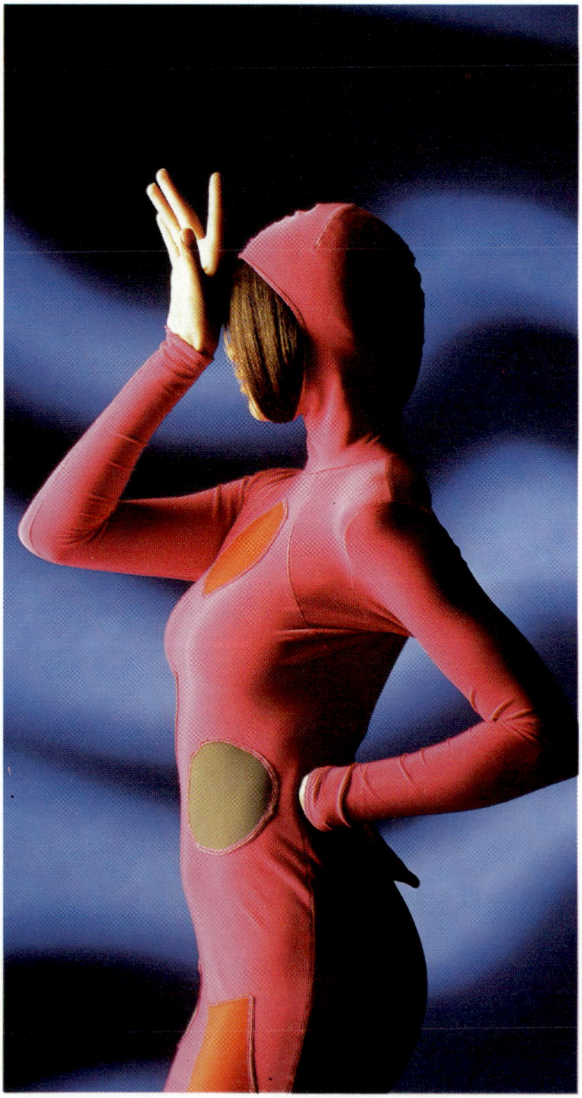

Why give a yarn a special name?

Although there are other elastic fibres similar to Lycra®, the exact formula for Lycra® is known only by Du Pont. It has been designed to be easy to wash, to resist wear from rubbing, and to accept heat and perspiration without damage.

Giving it a special name distinguishes it from other similar products, and tells you that it is of a guaranteed quality.

This type of advertisement is creating 'brand awareness'. The manufacturers want you to notice if you are using their product, and to look for it when you next go shopping.

8 Who wears Lycra®?

Lycra® and other similar yarns are worn by almost everyone. They are used in sports clothes and swimwear, in hosiery, and in the elastic that is put into waistbands.

In recent years elastane yarns have helped athletes to improve their speeds. They have also made athletes more comfortable, by providing long-lasting and strong elastic bandages which allow them to continue to play when they have had minor injuries.

These athletes are wearing garments designed to improve their performance. The garments are all made with Lycra® elastic yarns.

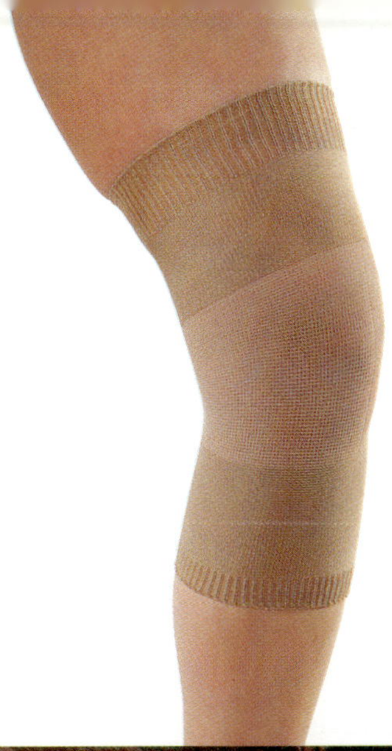

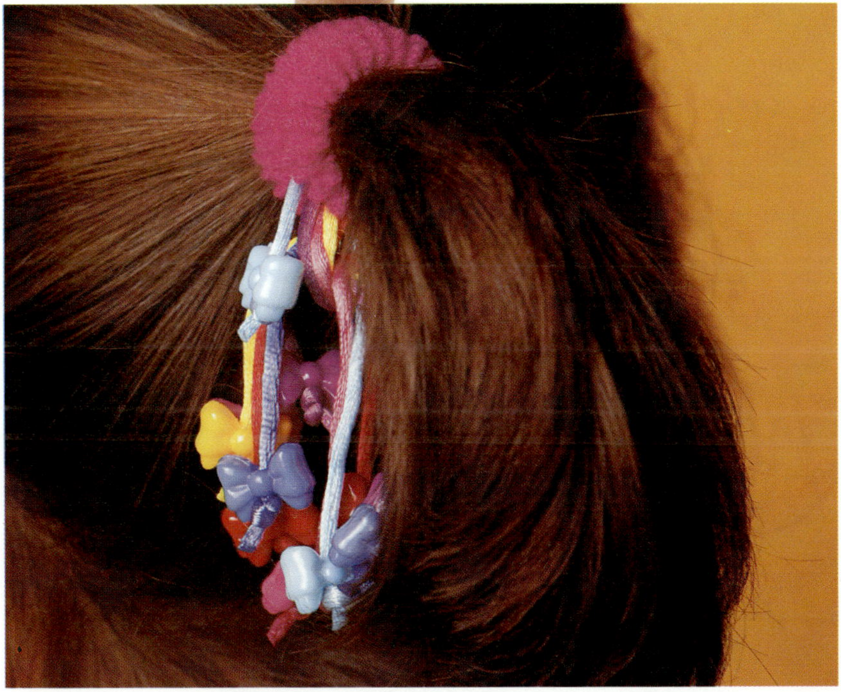

Many of the things that we wear have elastic in them.

Not just for sports

Ordinary people also wear a wide range of garments containing elastane and spandex yarns. Their popularity tells us that people like to be comfortable.

People want to wear things that fit well, but also allow them to move freely. Very tight clothes would be uncomfortable without elastic yarns.

9 Who wears leggings?

Leggings were first worn by dancers and people doing keep-fit programmes. Then they began to be seen at discos. Now most girls and women wear them.

At first leggings were worn only by people who needed to wear them. They were like a uniform, and identified the person wearing them as a dancer or as someone who was serious about keeping fit. During the 1980s people became very aware of fitness, and leggings were adopted as fashion garments. Clothes that become popular in this accidental way are called 'street fashion'.

At first fashion leggings were worn only by young people. They tend to wear new styles more quickly than older people.

Some people wear leggings indoors because they are practical and comfortable, but they may also choose to wear them outdoors.

Work clothes in fashion

Almost all the clothes that we wear most frequently began as garments for working people. For example, blue jeans were practical garments made for gold-miners and cowboys in the American West.

Originally, the people who wore jumpers were sailors and fishermen. So leggings are like many other garments that have become popular because they are practical.

10 Why are leggings Lycra®?

Leggings are practical, comfortable garments that fit closely, but they allow us to move freely. It is the elastic yarn, like Lycra®, that allows tight garments to move and not to go baggy.

Manufacturers make leggings containing Lycra® because they like to use a yarn that is good at doing its job. They also like to make garments that lots of people will buy. Using a yarn with a recognised name helps to do this, because it helps shoppers to find the leggings that will stretch and not go baggy, and that are long-lasting and easy to wash.

Up until about 400 years ago it was men who wore hose – tight, knitted garments.

Who can show their legs?

Before the Second World War, women did not wear trousers that showed the true shape of their legs. The development of elastic yarns made leggings available to male and female dancers over 30 years ago, but it was not until the 1980s that people accepted leggings as part of everyday female fashion.

Ideas can change a lot over the years: 400 years ago it was men who wore something like leggings, and women wore dresses down to the ground.

Tight trousers were fashionable in the late 1950s and in the 1960s, but they were not as tight as the stretch leggings of today.

Further information

The Marketing Manager
Du Pont UK Ltd
Textiles Fibres Division
94 Regent Road
Leicester LE1 7DJ

Booklet on Lycra® available on request.

The Plastics and Rubber Advisory Service
6 Bath Place
Rivington Street
London EC2A 3JE

Comprehensive information on all aspects of the plastics and rubber industry.

In your local shops, look for the special tags on garments containing Lycra®.

Glossary

Athletes — Athletes are people who play a lot of sports or games.

Core spinning — Core spinning is a way of making a stretchy yarn. A non-stretchy yarn is spun and at the same time it is wrapped around a stretchy yarn.

Covering — Covering is a way of putting a stretchy thread and non-stretchy thread together to make one yarn. This makes the whole yarn stretchy.

Elastane — Elastane is a very strong and stretchy fibre. It is made from a chemical which was first made in Germany about fifty years ago.

Elastic — Elastic things stretch and return to their original shape.

Fibres — Fibre is a general name for anything that can be made into yarn.

Garment — A garment is any piece of clothing.

Hosiery — Hosiery is a general name for all socks, stockings, and tights.

Latex — Latex is liquid rubber. It can be natural or chemical.

Lycra® — Lycra® is a trade name. It is an elastic fibre made by the Du Pont company. This is the only company which is allowed to use this name.

Spandex — Spandex is the word used in North America for elastane.

Stretchy — Stretchy things can be pulled out of shape.

Yarn — Yarn is a thick thread but it is thinner than rope.

Index

a b c d e f g h i j k l m n o p q r s t u v w x y z
A B C D E F G H I J K L M N O P Q R S T U V W X Y Z